AF559562

Ram Chalisa

Ram Chalisa

Published in Sanskriti Press
Rupa Publications India Pvt. Ltd 2025
161-B/4, Gulmohar House,
Yusuf Sarai Community Centre,
New Delhi 110049

Sales centres:
Bengaluru Chennai
Hyderabad Kolkata Mumbai

P-ISBN: 978-93-7003-761-8
E-ISBN: 978-93-7003-791-5

First impression 2025

10 9 8 7 6 5 4 3 2 1

Printed in India

Contents

Introduction

Shri Ram Chalisa is a revered devotional hymn composed in praise of **Lord Shri Ram**, the supreme embodiment of dharma, valour, compassion, and divine love. Recited by countless devotees across generations, this hymn captures the essence of Rama's divine personality—not only as the heroic prince of Ayodhya and the vanquisher of evil, but also as the eternal protector of those who seek refuge in Him with a pure heart.

Lord Rama the seventh incarnation of Lord Vishnu, stands as a timeless symbol of ideal human conduct. His life, as portrayed in the Ramayana, is a luminous path for mankind—teaching truth in speech, honour in relationships, humility in power, and unwavering devotion to duty. The Chalisa draws upon these divine qualities, describing His radiant form, sublime virtues, and the deep love He holds for His devotees.

Composed in forty verses (known as **chaupais**) along with a concluding pair of rhymed couplets (**dohas**), the Shri Ram Chalisa is traditionally attributed to **Goswami Tulsidas**, one of the greatest saints and poets of India's bhakti movement. Tulsidas, whose devotion to Lord Rama was unmatched, poured into this composition the yearning of the soul, the joy of surrender, and the power of divine remembrance.

The Chalisa does more than recount Lord Rama's glories—it brings the devotee into intimate proximity with the Lord. Each verse acts like a flower of devotion, offered at His lotus feet. As one chants these sacred lines, the mind is stilled, the heart softened, and the spirit uplifted. The beauty of the language, the rhythm of the meter, and the richness of imagery create a deep meditative experience, allowing the seeker to feel the living presence of Rama within.

In the Indian tradition, it is said that sincere recitation of the Shri Ram Chalisa removes fear, purifies the heart, dispels negativity, and grants inner strength to face life's challenges. It inspires righteousness, fills the soul with peace, and nurtures a sense of divine companionship that transcends all worldly sorrow. Over time, this regular devotion can become a bridge to spiritual liberation—a way to reach Lord Rama's eternal abode, where the soul rests in bliss.

Chalisa

।। चौपाई ।।

श्री रघुबीर भक्त हितकारी ।
सुनि लीजै प्रभु अरज हमारी ।।
निशि दिन ध्यान धरै जो कोई ।
ता सम भक्त और नहीं होई ।।

Shri Raghubir bhakt hitakari,
suni lijai prabhu araj hamari.
Nishi din dhyan dharae jo koi,
ta sam bhakt aur nahin hoi.

O Lord Raghubir (Rama), benefactor of devotees, please listen to my humble plea. Whoever meditates on You, day and night, no other devotee can match their greatness.

ध्यान धरें शिवजी मन मांही ।
ब्रह्मा, इन्द्र पार नहीं पाहीं ।।
दूत तुम्हार वीर हनुमाना ।
जासु प्रभाव तिहुं पुर जाना ।।

Dhyan dharen Shivji man maahi,
Brahma, Indra paar nahin paahi.
Doot tumhar veer Hanumana,
jasu prabhav tihun pur jana.

Even Lord Shiva meditates upon You
within his mind;
Yet Brahma, Indra, and others cannot fully
comprehend Your greatness.
Your messenger is the mighty Hanuman,
Whose glory is known throughout the
three worlds.

जय, जय, जय रघुनाथ कृपाला ।
सदा करो संतन प्रतिपाला ।।
तुव भुजदण्ड प्रचण्ड कृपाला ।
रावण मारि सुरन प्रतिपाला ।।

Jai, Jai, Jai Raghunath Kripala,
sada karo santan pratipala.
Tuv bhujdand prachand kripala,
Ravan mari suran pratipala.

Victory, victory, victory to You, O
compassionate Raghunath!
You always protect the saints and sages.
Your mighty arms are fierce and full of
mercy;
You slew Ravana and protected the gods.

तुम अनाथ के नाथ गोसाईं ।
दीनन के हो सदा सहाई ।।
ब्रह्मादिक तव पार न पावैं ।
सदा ईश तुम्हरो यश गावैं ।।

Tum anath ke nath Gosain,
dinan ke ho sada sahai.
Brahmadik tav paar na paave,
sada Ish tumharo yash gaave.

You are the guardian of the helpless, O Lord!
You are always the supporter of the downtrodden.
Even Brahma and others cannot reach the limits of Your glory;
All divine beings continuously sing Your praise.

चारिउ भेद भरत हैं साखी ।
तुम भक्तन की लज्जा राखी ।।
गुण गावत शारद मन माहीं ।
सुरपति ताको पार न पाहिं ।।

Charihu bhed Bharat hain sakhi,
tum bhaktan ki lajja rakhi.
Gun gavat Sharad man mahi,
Surpati tako paar na pahi.

The four Vedas and their essence bear witness,
That You always uphold the honor of Your devotees.
The goddess of learning, Saraswati, sings Your virtues in her heart;
Even the king of the gods (Indra) cannot comprehend them.

नाम तुम्हार लेत जो कोई ।
ता सम धन्य और नहीं होई ।।
राम नाम है अपरम्पारा ।
चारिहु वेदन जाहि पुकारा ।।

Naam tumhar let jo koi,
ta sam dhanya aur nahin hoi.
Ram naam hai aparmpara,
charihu vedan jahi pukara.

Whoever utters Your name,
There is no one more blessed than them.
The name of Rama is infinite and eternal,
It is hailed by all four Vedas.

गणपति नाम तुम्हारो लीन्हो ।
तिनको प्रथम पूज्य तुम कीन्हो ।।
शेष रटत नित नाम तुम्हारा ।
महि को भार शीश पर धारा ।।

Ganpati naam tumharo linho,
tinako pratham poojya tum kin ho.
Shesh ratat nit naam tumhara,
mahi ko bhar sheesh par dhara.

Even Lord Ganesha took Your name;
You made Him the first deity to be worshipped.
Sheshnaag continuously chants Your name,
Bearing the weight of the Earth on his head with ease.

फूल समान रहत सो भारा ।
पावत कोऊ न तुम्हरो पारा ।।
भरत नाम तुम्हरो उर धारो ।
तासों कबहूं न रण में हारो ।।

Phool saman rahat so bhara,
pavat kou na tumharo para.
Bharat naam tumharo ur dharo,
taso kabahun na rann mein haro.

That burden feels as light as a flower,
Yet no one can fathom Your greatness.
He who holds the name “Bharata” in his heart
Never loses in battle.

नाम शत्रुघ्न हृदय प्रकाशा ।
सुमिरत होत शत्रु कर नाशा ।।
लखन तुम्हारे आज्ञाकारी ।
सदा करत सन्तन रखवारी ।।

Naam Shatrughan hriday prakasha,
sumirat hot shatru kar nasha.
Lakhan tumhare agyakaari,
sada karat santan rakhwari.

The name 'Shatrughna' illumines the heart,
And by remembering it, enemies are destroyed.
Lakshman follows only Your commands;
He is ever the protector of the saints.

तातें रण जीते नहिं कोई ।

युद्ध जुरे यमहूं किन होई ।।

महालक्ष्मी धर अवतारा ।

सब विधि करत पाप को छारा ।।

Tate ran jeete nahin koi,
yuddh jure Yamahun kin hoi.
Mahalakshmi dhar avatara,
sab vidhi karat paap ko chhara.

Because of this, no one can defeat
You in battle;
Even Yama (god of death) avoids clashing
with You in war.
You manifested as Mahalakshmi,
Destroying all sin in every possible way.

सीता राम पुनीता गायो ।
भुवनेश्वरी प्रभाव दिखायो ।।
घट सों प्रकट भई सो आई ।
जाको देखत चन्द्र लजाई ।।

Sita Ram punita gayo,
Bhuvaneshwari prabhav dikhayo.
Ghat so prakat bhai so aai,
jako dekhat Chandra lajai.

You are praised as pure along with Sita,
Displaying the divine power of the
Goddess Bhuvaneshwari.
From a pot You manifested and appeared,
Even the moon felt shy in Your presence.

जो तुम्हरे नित पांव पलोटत ।
नवो निद्धि चरणन में लोटत ।।
सिद्धि अठारह मंगलकारी ।
सो तुम पर जावै बलिहारी ।।

Jo tumhare nit paanv palotat,
navo niddhi charanan mein lotat.
Siddhi atharah mangalkari,
so tum par jaave balihari.

At Your feet, those who bow every day,
Find the nine treasures lying there in surrender.
The eighteen auspicious siddhis (spiritual powers)
Are ever at Your command and serve You.

औरहु जो अनेक प्रभुताई ।
सो सीतापति तुमहिं बनाई ।।
इच्छा ते कोटिन संसारा ।
रचत न लागत पल की बारा ।।

Aurahu jo anek prabhutai,
so Sitapati tumhin banai.
Iccha te kotin sansara,
rachat na lagat pal ki bara.

All divine qualities and glories,
Belong to You, O consort of Sita.
You create countless universes at will,
And it doesn't even take You the time of a blink.

जो तुम्हरे चरणन चित लावै ।
ताकी मुक्ति अवसि हो जावै ।।
सुनहु राम तुम तात हमारे ।
तुमहिं भरत कुल पूज्य प्रचारे ।।

Jo tumhare charanan chit laave,
taki mukti avasi ho jaave.
Sunahu Ram tum tat hamare,
tumhin Bharat kul poojya prachare.

Whoever concentrates their mind at
Your feet,
They are surely liberated.
Listen, O Rama—You are our father and
protector!
You are the most revered of the Bharata
dynasty.

तुमहिं देव कुल देव हमारे ।
तुम गुरु देव प्राण के प्यारे ।।
जो कुछ हो सो तुमहिं राजा ।
जय जय जय प्रभु राखो लाजा ।।

Tumhin dev kul dev hamare,
tum guru dev pran ke pyare.
Jo kuchh ho so tumhin raja,
Jai Jai Jai prabhu rakho laja.

You are the supreme deity among all gods,
Our spiritual teacher and the dearest to
our souls.
Whatever exists, You alone are the king.
Victory, victory, victory, O Lord – please
protect our honour!

राम आत्मा पोषण हारे ।
जय जय जय दशरथ के प्यारे ।।
जय जय जय प्रभु ज्योति स्वरुपा ।
नर्गुण ब्रह्म अखण्ड अनूपा ।।

Ram atma poshan hare,
Jai Jai Jai Dasharath ke pyare.
Jai Jai Jai prabhu jyoti swarupa,
Nargun Brahma akhand anoopa.

You are the sustainer of all souls, O Rama,
Victory, victory, O beloved son of Dasharatha!
Victory to You, the embodiment of divine light,
Beyond attributes, eternal, unique, and complete!

सत्य सत्य जय सत्यव्रत स्वामी ।
सत्य सनातन अन्तर्यामी ।।
सत्य भजन तुम्हरो जो गावै ।
सो निश्चय चारों फल पावै ।।

Satya satya Jai Satyavrat Swami,
Satya Sanatan antaryami.
Satya bhajan tumharo jo gaave,
so nishchay charon phal paave.

Truth, truth, all glory to You,
Lord of Truth,
The eternal, all-knowing in dweller
of all hearts.
Whoever sings Your true devotion,
Surely obtains all four fruits of life
(Dharma, Artha, Kama, Moksha).

सत्य शपथ गौरीपति कीन्हीं ।
तुमने भक्तिहिं सब सिधि दीन्हीं ।।
ज्ञान हृदय दो ज्ञान स्वरुपा ।
नमो नमो जय जगपति भूपा ।।

Satya shapath Gauripati kinhi,
tumne bhaktihin sab sidhi dinhi.
Gyan hriday do gyan swarupa,
Namo Namo Jai Jagpati Bhoopa.

I swear on Lord Shiva's consort Parvati,
That You have granted all siddhis through devotion alone.
You are the embodiment of knowledge—grant us that wisdom;
We bow to You again and again, O Lord of the universe!

धन्य धन्य तुम धन्य प्रतापा ।
नाम तुम्हार हरत संतापा ।।
सत्य शुद्ध देवन मुख गाया ।
बजी दुन्दुभी शंख बजाया ।।

Dhanya dhanya tum dhanya pratapa,
naam tumhara harat santapa.
Satya shuddh devan mukh gaya,
baji dundubhi shankh bajaya.

Blessed, truly blessed is Your divine glory,
Your name alone removes all suffering.
The gods themselves have sung Your pure name;
The drums boomed and conch shells were blown in celebration.

सत्य सत्य तुम सत्य सनातन ।

तुम ही हो हमरे तन-मन धन ।।

याको पाठ करे जो कोई ।

ज्ञान प्रकट ताके उर होई ।।

Satya satya tum satya sanatan,
tum hi ho hamre tan-man dhan.
Yako paath kare jo koi,
gyan prakat take ur hoi.

Truly, truly, You are eternal truth;
You alone are our body, mind, and wealth.
Whoever reads this with faith and devotion,
Will awaken divine knowledge in their heart.

आवागमन मिटै तिहि केरा ।
सत्य वचन माने शिव मेरा ।।
और आस मन में जो होई ।
मनवांछित फल पावे सोई ।।

Aavagamana mitai tihi kera,
satya vachan mane Shiv mera.
Aur aas man mein jo hoi,
manvanchhit phal pave soi.

They will be freed from the cycle of birth and death,
This is the true promise of Lord Shiva.
And whatever desire remains in their heart,
They will attain it, no doubt.

तीनहुं काल ध्यान जो ल्यावै ।
तुलसी दल अरु फूल चढ़ावै ।।
साग पत्र सो भोग लगावै ।
सो नर सकल सिद्धता पावै ।।

Teenhun kaal dhyan jo lyavai,
tulsi dal aru phool chadhavai.
Saag patra so bhog lagaave,
so nar sakal siddhata paave.

If one remembers You at all three times
(morning, noon, night),
And offers tulsi leaves and flowers with
love,
Even with simple leafy vegetables as
offerings,
That person will gain all spiritual
awakenings.

अन्त समय रघुबर पुर जाई ।
जहां जन्म हरि भक्त कहाई ॥
श्री हरिदास कहै अरु गावै ।
सो बैकुण्ठ धाम को पावै ॥

Ant samay Raghubar pur jaai,
jahan janm Hari bhakt kahai.
Shri Haridas kahai aru gaave,
so Vaikunth dham ko paave.

At life's end, they shall go to the city of
Raghubar (Ayodhya),
Where birth as a true devotee of God is
granted.
Whoever sings and proclaims this as
Haridas (servant of God) has said,
Will surely attain the supreme abode—
Vaikuntha Dham.

॥ चौपाई ॥

सात दिवस जो नेम कर,पाठ करे चित लाय ।
हरिदास हरि कृपा से,अवसि भक्ति को पाय ॥
राम चालीसा जो पढ़े,राम चरण चित लाय ।
जो इच्छा मन में करै,सकल सिद्ध हो जाय ॥

Saat divas jo nem kar, paath kare chit laay.
Haridas Hari kripa se, avas bhakti ko paay.
Ram Chalisa jo padhe, Ram charan chit laay.
Jo ichchha man mein karai,
sakal siddh ho jaay.

He who observes discipline for seven days, and reads this with focused mind, By the grace of Lord Hari and Haridas, shall surely obtain devotion divine. He who recites the **Ram Chalisa**, with heart fixed at Rama's feet, Whatever desire lies in their mind, will be fulfilled, complete.

श्री राम आरती

श्री राम चंद्र कृपालु भजु मन हरण भव भय दारुणम्।
नव कंजलोचन, कंज-मुख, कर-कंज, पद कंजारुणम्।।

कन्दर्प अगणित अमित छवी नव नील नीरज सुन्दरम्।।
पट्पीत मानहु तडित रूचि शुचि नौमी जनक सुतावरम्।।

भजु दीनबंधु दिनेश दानव दैत्यवंश निकन्दनम्।
रघुनंद आनंद कंद कौशल चंद दशरथ नन्दनम्।।

सिर मुकुट कुंडल तिलक चारू उदारु अंग विभूषणं।
आजानु भुज शर चाप धर सग्राम जित खरदूषणं।।

इति वदित तुलसीदास शंकर-शेष-मुनि-मन रंजनम्।
मम ह्रदय-कंच निवास कुरु कामादि खलदल-गंजनम्।।

मनु जाहिं राचेउ मिलहि सो बरु सहज सुन्दर सांवरो।
करुना निधान सुजान सिलु सनेहु जानत रावरो।।

एही भांति गौरी असीस सुनी सिया सहित हियं हरषी अली।
तुलसी भवानी पूजी पुनी पुनी मन मन्दिर चली।।

दोहा

जानि गौरी अनुकूल सिय हिय हरषु ना जाइ ककहि।
मंजुल मंगल मूल बाम अंग फरकन लगे।।

Shri Ram Aarti

Shri Ram Chandra kripalu bhaju man
haran bhav bhay daarunam,
Nav kanjalochan, kanj-mukh,
kar-kanj, pad kanjaarunam.

Kandarp aganit amit chhavi
nav neel neeraj sundaram,
Patpeet maanahu tadit ruchi shuchi
naumi Janak sutavaram.

Bhaju deenabandhu Dinesh, daanav
daityavansh nikandanam,
Raghunand aanand kand Kaushal
chandra Dasharath nandanam.

Sir mukut kundal tilak chaaru,
udaaru ang vibhooshanam,
Aajaanu bhuj shar chaap dhar,
sangraam jit Khar-Dushanam.

Iti vadit Tulsidas, Shankar-
Shesh-muni-man ranjanam,
Mam hriday-kanch nivaas kuru,
kaamadi khaldal-ganjanam.

Manu jaahi raacheu milahi so baru,
sahaj sundar saanvaro,
Karuna nidhaan sujaan shil,
sanehu jaanat Raavaro.

Ehi bhaanti Gauri asees suni,
Siya sahit hiya harashi ali,
Tulsi Bhawani pooji puni,
puni man mandir chali.

Doha

Jaani Gauri anukool,
Siya hiya harashu na jaai kakhahi,
Manjul mangal mool,
baam ang pharkan lage.

O mind, adore and worship Lord Shri Ram Chandra, the compassionate one, Who removes the terrible fear of worldly existence (samsara).

His eyes are like newly bloomed lotus flowers,

His face, hands, and feet are lotus-like and radiantly red.

His beauty is countless times greater than that of millions of Cupids (Kamadevas),

Clad in yellow garments, He shines like a golden lightning streak—pure and splendid.

I bow to Him, the noble consort of Sita, the daughter of King Janak.

Worship the friend of the meek and the poor, the Sun among gods,

The destroyer of demons and evil beings.

He is the delight of the Raghu family, the source of bliss,

The moon of the Kaushal kingdom, and the beloved son of Dasharath.

With a crown upon His head, beautiful earrings, and a lovely tilak on His forehead,

His generous form is adorned with divine ornaments.

With long arms extending to His knees, holding a bow and arrows,

He conquered mighty demons like Khara

and Dushana in battle.

Thus speaks Tulsidas: He delights the minds of Lord Shankar, Sheshnag, and sages,

O Ram, please reside in the golden temple of my heart,

And destroy the evil tendencies like lust and pride.

Whom the mind truly longs for—

That rare and naturally beautiful, dark-complexioned Lord is attained.

The treasure of compassion, wise, humble,

And well aware of the depth of true love.

In this way, hearing the blessings of Goddess Gauri (Parvati),

Sita felt joy in her heart, and her friends rejoiced with her.

Tulsidas says: Sita worshipped Goddess Bhavani (Gauri) again and again,

And with a joyful heart, returned to the temple of her mind.

Doha (Couplet)

Knowing that Gauri (Parvati) is favorable and kind, Sita's heart was filled with boundless joy.

Her left limb (a sign of auspiciousness for women) began to twitch—A sign of beauty and the root of auspicious fortune.

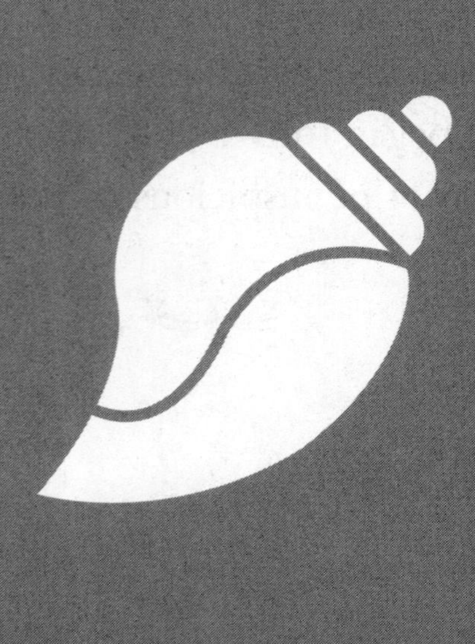